D0143131

Desert Climate

WEATHER AND CLIMATE

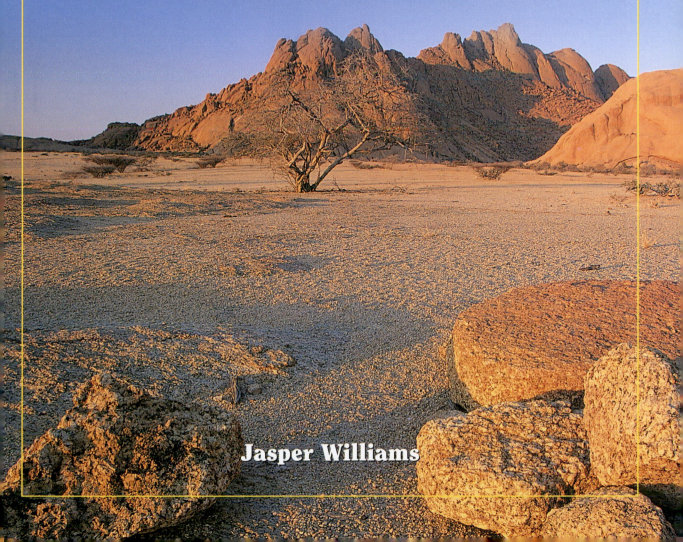

Jasper Williams

Produced through the worldwide resources of the National Geographic Society, John M. Fahey, Jr., President and Chief Executive Officer; Gilbert M. Grosvenor, Chairman of the Board.

PREPARED BY NATIONAL GEOGRAPHIC SCHOOL PUBLISHING
Sheron Long, Chief Executive Officer; Samuel Gesumaria, President; Steve Mico, Executive Vice President and Publisher; Francis Downey, Editor in Chief; Richard Easby, Editorial Manager; Margaret Sidlosky, Director of Design and Illustrations; Jim Hiscott, Design Manager; Cynthia Olson and Ruth Ann Thompson, Art Directors; Matt Wascavage, Director of Publishing Services; Lisa Pergolizzi, Production Manager.

MANUFACTURING AND QUALITY CONTROL
Christopher A. Liedel, Chief Financial Officer; Phillip L. Schlosser, Vice President; Clifton M. Brown III, Director.

EDITOR
Mary Anne Wengel

PROGRAM CONSULTANTS
Dr. Shirley V. Dickson, National Literacy Consultant; James A. Shymansky, E. Desmond Lee Professor of Science Education, University of Missouri-St Louis.

National Geographic Theme Sets program developed by Macmillan Education Australia Pty Limited.

Published by the National Geographic Society
1145 17th Street N.W.
Washington, D.C. 20036-4688

ISBN: 978-1-4263-5152-5

Printed in Hong Kong.

2011 2010 2009 2008 2007
3 4 5 6 7 8 9 10 11 12 13 14 15

Contents

Weather and Climate

Sunny, rainy, hot, windy, snowy. These are words people use to talk about the weather and the climate. But weather and climate are not the same. Weather is what happens in the air around us each day. Climate is the weather over a long period of time. Earth has four kinds of climate regions. These are polar, temperate, desert, and tropical.

 ## Key Concepts . . . .

1. Temperature, water in the air, and wind are some of the elements that make up weather.

2. Latitude, bodies of water, altitude, and winds are factors that affect climate.

3. Climate affects the way people live.

Four Kinds of Climates

Polar

Places with a polar climate are freezing cold all year.

Temperate

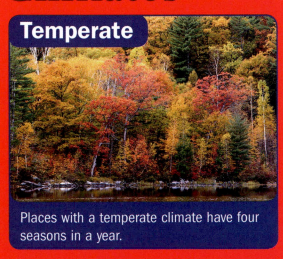

Places with a temperate climate have four seasons in a year.

In this book you will learn about weather and climate in desert regions.

Desert

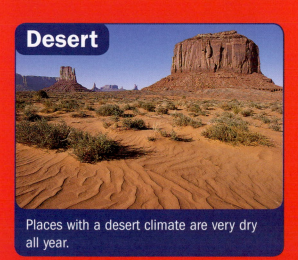

Places with a desert climate are very dry all year.

Tropical

Places with a tropical climate are warm and humid all year.

Desert Climate

Imagine living in a place that stays dry all year. There is almost no rain. Very few plants can grow. It is so hot that you cannot bear to stay outside for long. Or it is so cold that you need to wear warm clothes to survive. A place that receives very little rain or snow during the year has a desert climate. No matter how hot or cold a desert is, it will always be dry.

Desert Regions

Desert regions are extremely dry, or **arid.** They are found in areas on Earth that receive less than 25 centimeters (10 inches) of rain or snow each year.

This hot desert stays dry all year.

Deserts can be found in hot or cold places. Hot deserts are found in Africa, Asia, Australia, North America, and South America. Cold deserts are found in Antarctica, Asia, South America, and places near the Arctic. Both hot and cold deserts are dry.

The map below shows hot desert regions in yellow and cold desert regions in gray.

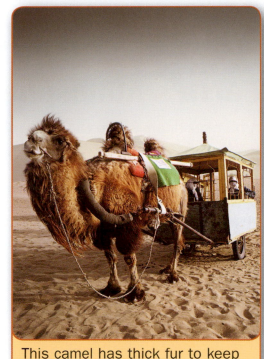

This camel has thick fur to keep it warm in the cold Gobi desert.

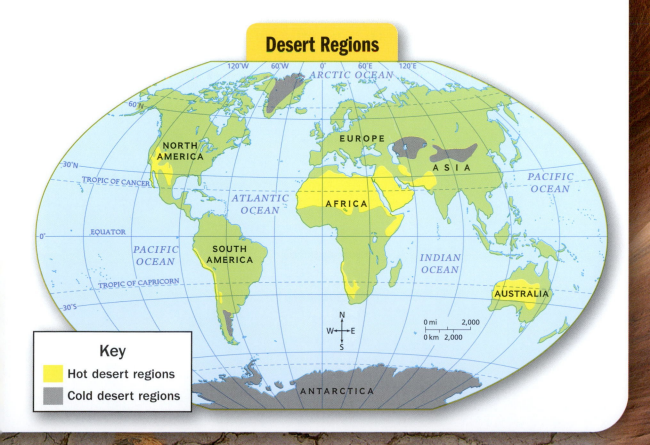

Desert Regions

120°W 60°W 0° 60°E 120°E

ARCTIC OCEAN

60°N

NORTH AMERICA

EUROPE

ASIA

PACIFIC OCEAN

30°N

TROPIC OF CANCER

ATLANTIC OCEAN

AFRICA

0°   EQUATOR

PACIFIC OCEAN

SOUTH AMERICA

INDIAN OCEAN

TROPIC OF CAPRICORN

AUSTRALIA

30°S

N
W E
S

0 mi   2,000
0 km 2,000

Key
Hot desert regions
Cold desert regions

ANTARCTICA

Key Concept 1 Temperature, water in the air, and wind are some of the elements that make up weather.

Earth's Atmosphere

A blanket of air called the **atmosphere** surrounds Earth. The atmosphere is made up of dust, water, and gases such as nitrogen and oxygen. The atmosphere has five layers. These five layers are the troposphere, stratosphere, mesosphere, thermosphere, and exosphere.

Weather takes place in the troposphere. The troposphere is 10–16 kilometers (6–10 miles) thick. It is the layer of atmosphere closest to Earth.

weather
the state of the atmosphere at a time and place

Layers of the Atmosphere

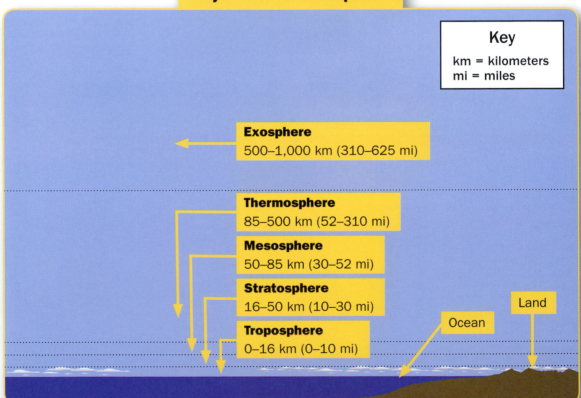

Key
km = kilometers
mi = miles

Exosphere
500–1,000 km (310–625 mi)

Thermosphere
85–500 km (52–310 mi)

Mesosphere
50–85 km (30–52 mi)

Stratosphere
16–50 km (10–30 mi)

Troposphere
0–16 km (0–10 mi)

Ocean

Land

Weather

The weather of a place changes as the air changes. Air can be warm or cool, and wet or dry. Moving air is called wind. **Temperature,** water in the air, and wind are elements that make up weather.

temperature
the measure of how hot or cold a place is

Temperature Not all places on Earth have the same temperature. This is because the sun's rays heat some places more than others. Earth's surface is curved, so the rays hit some places more directly than others. Places near the **Equator** get a lot of direct sunlight. They have warm temperatures all year round. Places near the Poles get less direct sunlight. They have cold temperatures all year round.

Earth's hot deserts are in areas just north and south of the Equator. Many cold deserts, such as Antarctica, are closer to Earth's Poles.

Heat from the Sun

North Pole

Equator

South Pole

Sun's rays are spread out.

Sun's rays are direct.

Water in the Air The amount of water in the air affects weather. The sun's rays heat water on Earth's surface. The heat causes the water to change into a gas called water vapor. The water vapor mixes with the air. Water changing into gas is called **evaporation.**

The warm air from Earth's surface rises and mixes with cool air in the troposphere. When this happens, the water vapor cools and turns back into drops of water. Water vapor changing into water is called **condensation.** The drops of water join together to form clouds. As the water drops get bigger, the clouds get heavier. The water from the clouds then falls back to Earth as rain, snow, sleet, or hail. These are all forms of **precipitation.** Desert regions get very little precipitation.

The Water Cycle

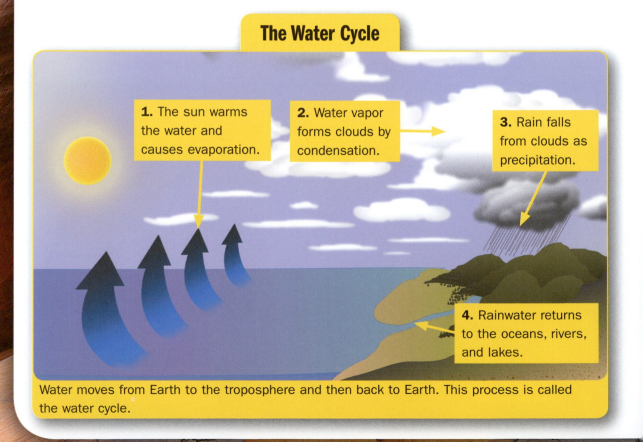

1. The sun warms the water and causes evaporation.

2. Water vapor forms clouds by condensation.

3. Rain falls from clouds as precipitation.

4. Rainwater returns to the oceans, rivers, and lakes.

Water moves from Earth to the troposphere and then back to Earth. This process is called the water cycle.

Wind Wind is moving air. Air moves all the time, but you do not always feel this movement. But when a lot of air moves from one place to another, you can feel it. This is called wind.

All the air around Earth has weight. The weight of air pressing down on Earth is called **air pressure.** Air pressure is not always the same. The weight of air depends on its temperature. Warm air is lighter than cold air. Warm air rises. As warm air rises, it creates an area of low air pressure.

Cold air is heavier than warm air. Cold air sinks and pushes with greater force on Earth. This creates an area of high air pressure. Air always moves from areas of high air pressure to areas of low air pressure. This movement causes wind.

Wind in the desert can cause a sandstorm.

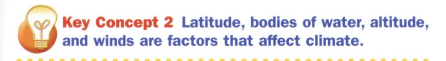

Climate

Climate is the pattern of weather in a place over a long period of time. In most regions, weather follows a similar pattern year after year.

> *climate*
> the type of weather a place experiences over a long time

Places that have a desert climate receive less than 25 centimeters (10 inches) of precipitation each year. They can be hot or cold deserts. The Sahara desert in Africa is a hot desert. Antarctica is a cold desert. Both are dry all year round.

Several factors affect the climate of a place. These factors include latitude, bodies of water, altitude, and prevailing winds.

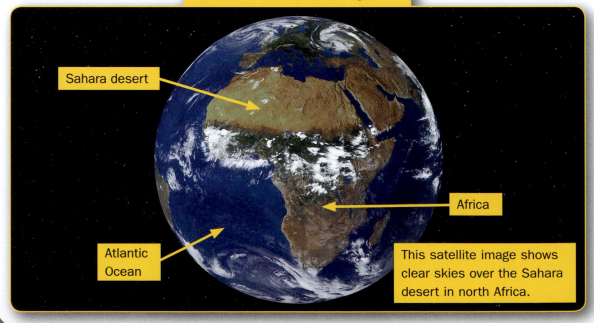

View of Earth from Space

Sahara desert

Africa

Atlantic Ocean

This satellite image shows clear skies over the Sahara desert in north Africa.

Latitude Latitude measures how far north or south a place is from the Equator. Latitude is measured in degrees. The Equator is at 0° latitude. The farther away a place is from the Equator, the higher its latitude.

Latitude affects the temperature of a place. This is because the sun's rays strike Earth differently at different latitudes. The sun's rays strike most directly at the Equator. It is hot here all year round. Places at higher latitudes receive less direct sun. In these places, the sun's rays strike Earth's surface at an angle. The heat here is less intense.

Hot, moist air from the Equator loses its moisture as it moves north and south. By the time it reaches about 23.5° north or south, the air is dry. The dry air helps create desert climates in these places.

Degrees of Latitude

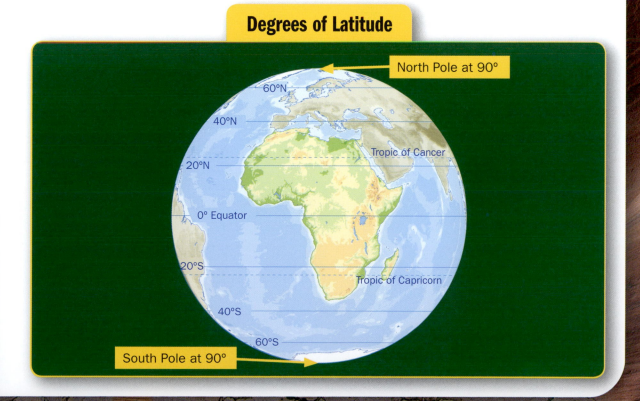

North Pole at 90°
60°N
40°N
Tropic of Cancer
20°N
0° Equator
20°S
Tropic of Capricorn
40°S
60°S
South Pole at 90°

Large Bodies of Water Large bodies of water, such as oceans, affect climate. Water in oceans evaporates and then condenses. This causes precipitation.

Many deserts are far from oceans. The air in these deserts is dry because it does not have much water vapor.

Even deserts near oceans are dry. The Sahara desert in Africa is close to the Atlantic Ocean. But the air here is dry. This is because the movement of air creates an area of low air pressure over this desert. Hot, moist air rises near the Equator. It quickly drops its moisture as rain. By the time this air reaches the Sahara, it is dry. The dry air forms an area of low air pressure and stops clouds from forming. This keeps the Sahara hot and dry.

Some parts of the Sahara get less than 2.5 centimeters (1 inch) of rain a year.

Altitude Altitude is the measure of how high a place is above sea level. Altitude is measured in meters (feet). It affects climate because it affects air pressure. High-altitude areas have low air pressure. As altitude increases, the air pressure drops and the air cools.

Places at high altitudes, such as mountains, have cold climates, no matter where they are located. This means mountains near the Equator will have cold temperatures.

A **montane** desert is a desert that occurs at a high altitude. Not much grows in montane deserts because these places are very cold and dry.

This montane desert in India stays cold and dry throughout the year.

Prevailing Winds Prevailing winds are winds that blow most often in the same direction. Prevailing winds carry warm air from the Equator and cool air from the Poles. These winds blow huge masses of air over Earth. They affect climate all over Earth.

Prevailing winds do not blow directly north or south. They are forced east and west as Earth rotates. The prevailing winds that blow over Earth's desert regions are known as **trade winds.** Trade winds drive away clouds as they move toward the Equator. More sunlight can then reach the land. The Sahara desert can become very hot because of the effect of trade winds.

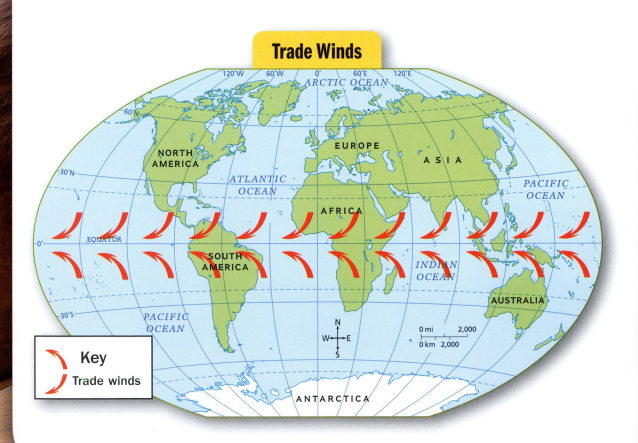

Trade Winds

People and Climate

People around the world live in different climates. They have learned to **adapt** to the climate they live in. Climate affects the way people live. It affects the homes they build, the food they eat, the way they dress, and the jobs they do.

Living in a desert climate can be difficult. Water is always scarce. There are few building materials people can use to build houses. People must live with the resources the environment provides.

A Bedouin sits in the doorway of his dry-mud house in Morocco.

Many people who live in desert regions move from place to place in search of food and water. They live in huts and tents made of animal skin. They take their homes with them when they move.

People who live in hot desert regions wear loose-fitting clothes to stay cool and protect themselves from the sun.

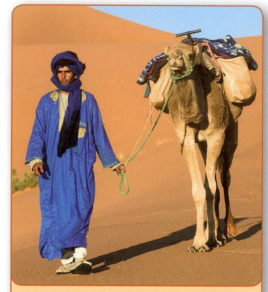

This man is wearing traditional, loose-fitting clothes to keep him cool in the desert.

Many people in the Gobi desert live in yurts. These are tents that can be taken down easily and carried when it is time to move to a new place.

Think About the **Key Concepts**

Think about what you read. Think about the pictures and diagrams. Use these to answer the questions. Share what you think with others.

1. What are three elements that make up the weather of a place?

2. Why does the weather of a place change from day to day?

3. How is climate different from weather?

4. How does the climate of a place affect the lives of the people who live there?

Satellite Image

Satellite images are photographs taken from space.
Look back at the satellite image on page 12. It is a satellite image of Earth. It shows weather conditions over the Sahara desert in Africa.

Satellite images help you study the weather and climate of a place.
The photograph on page 21 is also a satellite image. It shows the weather conditions in northwest Africa. To study the satellite image, follow the steps below.

How to Study a Satellite Image

1. Read the title.
The title tells you what the image shows.

2. Read the labels.
The labels name different parts of the image.

3. Study the satellite image.
Think about what the satellite image shows.

4. Think about what you have learned.
What does the brownish patch on the Atlantic show?

Northwest Africa

Atlantic Ocean

SAHARA DESERT

Winds carrying sand

Thin cloud

Study the Satellite Image

Study the satellite image by following the steps on page 20.
Write down all the things you learned about the weather conditions
in northwest Africa. Share what you learned with a classmate.

News Report

A **news report** gives information about current events. You may read news reports in newspapers or magazines. The report starting on page 23 tells about the spreading of deserts.

A news report includes the following:

The **headline** tells what the report is about. It makes the reader want to read on.

The **lead** gives the reader the most important information in a sentence or short paragraph.

The **body paragraphs** develop the report. They may provide background information and many interesting facts.

Photographs, maps, or **diagrams** show you what you are reading about.

Captions say what is happening in the photographs.

New Delhi, July 20

Global Warming Is Spreading Seas of Sand

The **date** tells when the report was written.

The **headline** tells what the report is about.

The **lead** gives the most important facts in a sentence or two.

Photographs, maps, or **diagrams** show you what you are reading about.

Scientists fear that New Delhi, India, could soon be overrun by the Thar Desert. They also say parts of Africa could become vast seas of sand by 2050. They blame global warming.

Global warming is the warming of Earth's atmosphere. It happens because harmful gases in the atmosphere are increasing. Gases exist in the atmosphere, naturally. Like a greenhouse, these gases trap heat. They help keep Earth warm. Scientists call this the greenhouse effect.

One of the greenhouse gases is carbon dioxide. Burning fuels, such as coal and oil, releases carbon dioxide. This increases the levels of gas in the atmosphere. The extra gas traps too much heat. This contributes to global warming on Earth.

The Thar Desert may expand and, in time, cover India's capital, New Delhi.

Captions say what is happening in the photographs.

Body paragraphs develop the topic.

23

Global Warming and Deserts

Subheads break the topics into easy-to-find sections.

Global warming is making places on Earth hotter and drier. Most plants cannot grow in a hot, dry climate. When plants die, their roots no longer hold the soil in place. The soil turns into dust and sand.

In many areas, good land is turning into desert. Deserts can spread. Over time, winds can blow sand into the greener areas. The sand can bury any plants growing there.

People also cause deserts to spread. When people cut down trees or let their cattle overgraze, the soil can become loose and dry. It is easily blown away by the wind. Plants cannot grow on the land. The land turns into desert.

The Spreading Thar Desert

Research shows the Thar Desert in India is spreading by about .5 kilometers (.3 miles) a year. The Thar Desert covers 199,430 square kilometers (77,000 square miles) of land. If it continues to spread, it may soon cover many towns and cities.

Global warming is making parts of India hotter and drier. Recently, there have been more droughts here. Droughts affect farmers. They cannot grow enough crops to feed people.

Sandstorms, such as this one in the Kalahari Desert, blow loose dust and sand into the air.

The Spreading Kalahari Desert

Deserts are spreading in other parts of the world. Global warming is likely to affect deserts in Africa as well. Less rain will cause deserts such as the Kalahari to spread. The Kalahari Desert is in southern Africa. It covers 500,000 square kilometers (190,000 square miles). If the dry conditions continue, the Kalahari Desert is likely to expand. Land that is now green will become dry. It will become desert.

People raise livestock at the edge of the Kalahari Desert. Too many animals are grazing there. Plants have no time to grow again. With fewer plants holding the soil together, it becomes loose and unstable. Loose soil is easily blown away by wind. With no soil, it is difficult for plants to grow. This causes the land to become desert.

If the desert expands, there will be less food for livestock. Many people who depend on livestock for food and income will be affected.

Desert Regions

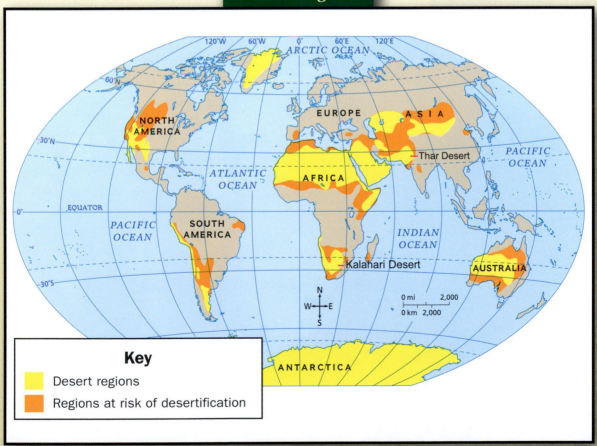

Key
- Desert regions
- Regions at risk of desertification

How Can We Help?

The spreading of deserts threatens one-quarter of Earth's land. It could affect the lives of nearly 900 million people. It is a serious problem.

Expanding deserts are linked to global warming. Some scientists think it is too late to stop global warming. But others think we can stop it from getting worse.

One way is to limit the use of fuels, such as coal and oil, that give off greenhouse gases. People can buy cars that use less gas. Countries around the world need to work together to find solutions to this problem.

People can work to prevent the spread of deserts too. They can stop cutting down forests for farmland. There are many things they can do to help.

These people are working to stop the illegal logging of forests in Africa.

Apply the Key Concepts

Key Concept 1 Temperature, water in the air, and wind are some of the elements that make up weather.

Activity

Make a list of the elements of weather. Use the Internet or library to find out what instruments people use to measure the elements of weather. Add the names of the instruments to your list of weather elements. Draw the instruments and label them.

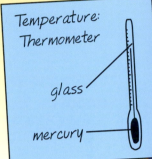

Temperature: Thermometer

glass

mercury

Key Concept 2 Latitude, bodies of water, altitude, and winds are factors that affect climate.

Activity

Draw a picture that shows the climate you have read about. Label the parts of your picture. Write a caption that explains how where you live is similar to or different from the climate you have read about.

New York in summer. . .

Key Concept 3 Climate affects the way people live.

Activity

Think of the different ways in which climate affects your life. For example, you may need to wear warm clothes during some months of the year. Draw two different ways you have adapted to the climate.

Warm Clothing

RESEARCH AND WRITE

Write
Your Own
News Report

You have read the news report about the spreading of deserts. Now it is time to write your own news report about the environment.

1. Study the Model

Look back at the news report on pages 23–26. Find the important features of a news report. Think about how the headline tells what the report is about and makes it sound interesting. Think about the information contained in the first paragraph. Read the body text again. Note the detailed information.

Writing a News Report
- Choose a current event or topic in the news.
- Use a headline that grabs readers' attention.
- Write the most important information in the lead.
- Develop the topic in the body of the report.

2. Choose Your Topic

Now think about a topic you can write your report about. The report should be about a current event or topic in the news. It should have to do with the environment. You may choose to write about damage or threats to the environment. Or you may choose to write about how people are working to protect the environment. Read newspapers and search the Internet for ideas for a topic. Look for a topic that interests you.

3. Research Your Topic

Write down a list of questions that you will answer in your article. Think of who, what, when, where, why, and how questions. Research your topic to answer your questions. Take notes. Write down any interesting facts you find. Look for pictures and diagrams to include in your report.

Topic: Drought

1. What causes drought?

2. Which parts of the world are affected by drought?

4. Write a Draft

Put your notes in an order that makes sense. Then write a draft of your report. Remember to put the most important information in the first paragraph. It should not be longer than a sentence or two. Add more detailed information in the body text. Include interesting facts.

5. Revise and Edit

Read your draft. Make corrections as you go. Double check all dates, times, or other facts against your research. Make sure all names are spelled correctly.

When you are happy with your report, write a headline. Make sure it describes the topic of your report in a few words and makes people want to keep reading.

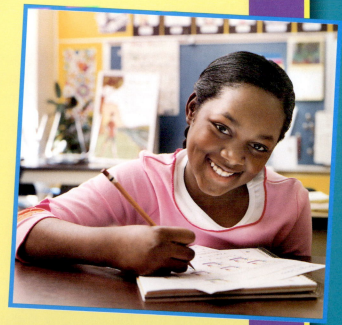

Create a Magazine of News Reports

Now you can get together with the rest of the class to create a magazine of news reports.

How to Make a News Magazine

1. Look at a news magazine.
Read the contents page and find the articles or reports. Look at how they are arranged on the pages.

2. Type your news report.
Type your news report into two columns and print it out.

3. Find a photograph to go with your news report.
Print a photograph or two from the Internet, or photocopy one from a newspaper or news magazine. The photograph should show what your news report is about. Paste the photograph under your report.

4. Write a caption for your photograph.
The caption will say what is happening in the photograph. The caption should relate to the report.

5. Put the news magazine together.
Put all the class news reports together. Number the pages.

6. Create a contents page.
Write a list of the news reports in the order they appear in the magazine. Write the page number next to the name of each report.

7. Create a cover.
Choose a name for your news magazine and write it on the cover. Choose a good photograph from one of the news reports that you can copy and paste on the cover.

Glossary

adapt – change to suit a particular situation

air pressure – the weight of air pressing down on Earth

arid – dry

atmosphere – the layers of gases that surround Earth

climate – the type of weather a place experiences over a long time

condensation – the process of a gas changing to a liquid

Equator – an imaginary line around Earth that separates the Northern Hemisphere from the Southern Hemisphere

evaporation – the process of a liquid changing to a gas

montane – mountainous

precipitation – water that falls to Earth as rain, snow, sleet, or hail

temperature – the measure of how hot or cold a place is

trade winds – easterly winds blowing from high pressure areas in the subtropics to low pressure areas at the Equator

weather – the state of the atmosphere at a time and place

Index